THE
SEMINOLE

by Barbara Brooks

Illustrated by Luciano Lazzarino

ROURKE PUBLICATIONS, INC.

VERO BEACH, FLORIDA 32964

CONTENTS

Library of Congress Cataloging-in-Publication Data

Brooks, Barbara 1946–
   The Seminoles / by Barbara Brooks.
      p.   cm. —(Native American people)
   Summary: Examines the history, traditional lifestyle, and current situation of the Seminole Indians.
      1. Seminole Indians—Juvenile literature.   [1. Seminole Indians.   2. Indians of North America.]   I. Title.   I. Series.
   E99.S28B76 1989   975.9'00497—dc19
         ISBN 0-86625-377-7

88-6920

INTRODUCTION

Many names of places such as Tallahassee, Okeechobee and Miami remind Florida residents of their Indian ancestors. The peninsula was home for many Native Americans before the white man arrived. Impressive burial mounds are found along the coast and rivers. The mounds date back thousands of years.

About 12,000 years ago when the great Ice Age was drawing to a close, the first people entered Florida. They were descendants from groups of people thought to have migrated across a land bridge connecting the continents of Asia and North America. Today we recognize these people as the first true native Americans. Columbus called them Indians because he thought he had reached India. Indians have features similar to the peoples of China and Japan.

The first Florida Indians were hunters and gatherers. They used flesh for food, skins for clothing and bones for tools. They ate wild plants and nuts.

At the beginning of the Christian era, Indians occupied the entire peninsula and the Florida Keys. The Indians had evolved a long way from their primitive nomadic way of life. They lived in large communities and traded at great distances. A relatively complex government and social class system had developed.

The behavior of the white man often determined whether these Indians were hostile or friendly. Many Florida tribes resisted the Spanish explorers violently. Eventually the original tribes were wiped out through war, disease and slavery.

As the original Florida tribes disappeared, Creek Indians and black slaves from Alabama and Georgia moved into Florida wanting to get away from the

Leg rattles from box turtle shells worn for the Green Corn Dance.

American colonists and traders. The Spanish encouraged this migration because they knew they needed a supporting population north of St. Augustine.

The migration of these bands lasted over a period of one hundred years. Some were lower Creeks, some were the rival upper Creeks. The Creek culture was their common bond. These migrating Indians were called the Seminoles which comes from a Creek Indian word "isti simanole." Translated, that means "runaway, wild, and untamed." Indians say it also means "freedom."

As the white settlers pushed further into Florida, the Seminoles were driven further south. The U.S. government treated the Seminoles dishonestly and vicious wars plagued the land until 1851. Many Seminoles were forced to leave Florida and move to a territory that later became Oklahoma. Their descendants live there today.

The surviving Florida Seminoles hid deep in the swamps living in isolation without ever making peace with the United States. Today the descendants of these unconquered people live in a variety of old and new ways. Although the Seminoles are rather new as a tribe, they have developed their own culture and customs.

The Seminoles

Indian
Territory

← Seminole
Resettlement

Creek
↓
Seminole

Apalachee

Timucua

Calusa

Seminole

Tekesta

Sometimes baskets were made for a specific purpose. Top: The weaving of the corn flour basket is tight so none of the flour is lost. Left: A corn sifting basket is loosely woven so that foreign matter will drop out, leaving only corn. Right: An all-purpose utility basket.

(Photo courtesy The St. Lucie County Historical Museum)

The Original Florida Indians

AROUND 15,000 Indians were living in Florida when the Spanish first landed in April 1513. There were four major tribes called Calusa, Tekesta, Timucua, and Apalachee. These were organized into fifty smaller bands. The Spanish found it difficult to settle in the southwest of Florida and on the state's east coast because the Indians were very hostile.

The Calusa (ka LOO sa) lived along the Gulf Coast of Florida. They were mariners and fishermen. No Spanish settlement was ever established in this area because the Indians successfully repelled the invaders. The famous Spanish explorer, Ponce de León, died of a wound inflicted by a Calusa arrow.

The largest group of Florida Indians were the Timucua (ti MOO coo ah) and Tekesta (ta KESS ta), both of whom lived on the east Florida coast. They farmed and fished. Like the Calusa, they were also fierce warriors intent on stopping the Spanish.

In northern Florida lived the Apalachee (ap a LAY chee). These Indians were friendlier. They were mostly farmers. Their culture was further advanced than the other Florida tribes. The Spanish were able to establish a string of settlements from St. Augustine to Tallahassee. For almost one hundred years these Indians lived in peace with the white man.

All the Florida Indians were doomed to extinction. The white man took what he wanted ruthlessly, without regard for the rights of the natives. Eventually almost the entire Florida Indian population was wiped out by diseases they caught from the white man and in wars.

The Creek Indians and Blacks Move to Florida

At various times over the centuries, England and Spain had been at war with each other in Europe. As the English settled in the Carolinas and Georgia, the struggle between these two nations revived. In the early 1700s, Florida became a place of conflict. The Creek Indians of Georgia sided with the English. They killed many Florida Indians and sold others to slave traders in Charleston. There the Indians were sold to plantation owners.

The empty land was rich for farming and hunting. Soon the Creek invaders began to settle into northern Florida. Other Creek tribes from the Carolinas, Alabama, and Georgia moved to Florida, too. They were trying to escape white settlements. Many had been made slaves and were escaping from their captors.

Black runaway slaves also sought new homes in Florida. All these new people mixed with the survivors of the original tribes of Florida. They banded together, since they were facing similar problems and needed to seek Spanish protection. They were called the Seminoles.

The Seminoles in the 1700s

Living on the richest land in the area, the Seminoles of the 1700s were hard working and prosperous. They hunted, fished, and raised crops and livestock. Skins, furs, dried fish, beeswax, honey, and bear oil were traded to the Spanish for coffee, sugar, tobacco, and liquors.

Their towns were designed like the Creek villages. A town square and community building was surrounded by thirty homes. The buildings were made from logs. Each home consisted of two houses about twenty yards apart. One of these units was two stories, and used for food storage. A one-story building nearby was used for cooking and sleeping.

Each family had a personal garden with corn, beans, and melons. There also was a common plantation farmed by the whole village. The people contributed to the public food supply for visitors and less fortunate members of the tribe.

The Seminoles followed the Creek political system. There were two types of chiefs, a peace chief and a war chief. In some clans, the position of peace chief was partly inherited, and the peace chief served also as religious leader in tribal ceremonies. Each town was independent of other Seminole communities. No chief ruled all the towns.

A tribal council made up of the oldest and wisest men helped the peace chief rule. The council elected the war chiefs. They were also responsible for the safety and welfare of all the people in a town. During wartime, chiefs were selected for their military ability and leadership skills. A man who spoke clearly and convincingly could win a high position.

Many blacks worked for the Seminoles. Some were slaves, but they were treated like tenant farmers. These blacks prospered and soon some owned their own farms, had their own villages, and elected their own chiefs. Some married Seminoles. The blacks and the Seminoles banded together against the white man.

7

First Seminole War

After the Revolutionary War, there was conflict between the United States and Spain. The Seminoles continued to welcome black slaves who ran away from plantations in the United States. The Spanish usually accepted the runaway slaves as free citizens. This made the plantation owners angry. They tried to invade the Indian villages to get their slaves back. The Indians strongly resisted. Hatred grew between the plantation owners and the Seminoles.

Increasing clashes led to the First Seminole War in 1818. General Andrew Jackson was sent to Florida with 3,000 men. Jackson attacked the Seminoles, burning most of their towns and taking their food. Great numbers of their horses

and hogs were taken, and their cattle driven away. Jackson killed or captured all that stood in his way. Spanish settlements were also attacked.

Florida was ceded to the United States in 1819. In the treaty, Spain asked that the people of Florida be accepted as citizens of the United States. The United States agreed to this, but they considered only the Spanish the people of Florida. The Indians and Negroes were not included as citizens. They were people of a different color and way of living. The white man thought they were inferior and not entitled to freedom and justice. At this time, the Seminole population was approximately 5,000 persons.

The Struggle to Survive

Florida became a territory of the United States in 1822. General Jackson became the first military governor of Florida. He soon resigned when he failed to get support of his policies. William P. Duval followed Jackson as governor. He was a fair and honest man, well-liked by the Indians and the whites. Keeping peace between the new settlers and the Seminoles was a huge task for him.

The thousands of settlers who began to move to Florida wanted the rich Indian land. They began to demand that all the Seminoles be sent to the Indian Territory in the western part of United States. It was Governor Duval's job to move the Seminoles to inferior lands below Tampa Bay in Florida, or convince them to move west.

Through a treaty in 1823, the Seminoles agreed to give up 32 million acres of the rich, fertile land in northern Florida. The governor told the Seminoles that they would no longer be permitted to roam throughout Florida. They would have an assigned territory on a reservation of 4 million acres in central Florida.

The Seminoles had to leave their villages and fertile lands for a place in the middle of the state. It was not near either coast. The intent was to cut off their supply of gunpowder, ammunition, and arms from Cuba to prevent another war. The treaty provided that whites could not hunt, settle, or intrude on Seminole lands.

The next few years brought hardship to the Seminoles. The sudden and drastic change in their lifestyle was difficult. The Seminoles struggled to survive. They rebuilt their homes and dug canals where the land was too swampy for trails. They cleared patches of land for their cornfields and vegetable gardens and raised cattle. They found it impossible to grow enough food to support their people. The soil was poor, waterlogged, and not well suited for farming. Good drinking water was hard to find. The chiefs complained about the absence of game and of fruit and nuts. Tormented by hunger, the Indians raided white settlements for food. The Florida government then passed a law forbidding Indian men from leaving the reservation without written permission.

White men broke the treaty, raiding the Seminole villages for black slaves who had been living among the Seminoles for years. Demands from the white settlers to send the Indians west added to the conflict.

Second Seminole War

In May 1830, President Andrew Jackson signed the Indian Removal Act. All the Indians of the Southeast were to be moved across the Mississippi River into the Indian Territory, land set aside specifically for Indians. Indian Territory later became the State of Oklahoma. This was a blow to the Seminoles, who refused to move again. Tension mounted, and treaties were drawn and broken by both sides. Representatives from the United States government tried to convince the Seminoles that the new territory would be better for them than the reservation in Florida.

The Seminoles agreed to send several chiefs to look over the region and bring a report back to their people. The group spent three months on their inspection. While on the tour of the proposed new

reservation, some of the chiefs were convinced to sign another treaty. This treaty said that the Seminoles had three years to move out of Florida. It has been said the chiefs were bribed into signing this treaty.

When the Seminoles found out about this treaty, they were very angry. They felt betrayed, and refused to agree to its terms. For leadership they looked to a chief named Osceola. He believed that the Florida land belonged to his people.

Osceola was not a chief by birth, but his courage to speak out against the whites made him respected by his people. He was born in Georgia in 1804. There are stories that Osceola had mixed blood, but he always claimed he was a pure-blood Muskogee. His influence and power was great among the Seminoles. Their legends remember him as one of their fearless war heroes. He fought for principles that he thought were just and right for his people.

Representatives of the United States

met with the Seminole chiefs in May 1835. They insisted the Indians must move or troops would force them out. Osceola stepped forward to the council table, plunged a knife into the treaty, and said the Seminoles would not move. It was an open declaration of war.

The Second Seminole War began in 1835. It would continue for seven bitter years. There were many battles between the United States and the Seminoles. Often the Indians were successful because they knew the land well. They could attack the white soldiers by surprise and then disappear into the swamps. Osceola was feared and respected. It was difficult for the white soldiers to defeat him.

In 1837, after two years of fierce fighting, Osceola agreed to talk peace under a flag of truce. It turned out to be a dishonorable trick. Osceola was captured and thrown into prison. With his spirit broken, he became ill in prison and died in 1838.

The Seminoles are Forced to Move

The war dragged on. After eight long years of fighting, many Seminoles had been killed. Others were caught and sent west. About 3,000 Seminoles were forced to migrate to the Indian Territory.

The trip was difficult and is often called the "Trail of Tears." Forced to leave their homes, campfires, and fields, they plodded west. Few white people understood their fierce attachment to the burial grounds of their ancestors and the homes of their childhood. Now they lived in very crowded conditions with little food. Many got sick and died.

When they arrived in Indian Territory, the Seminoles were expected to become part of the Creek nation. But the Seminoles wanted to govern themselves and have their own land. There were many conflicts between the Seminoles and the Creeks. A treaty was signed in 1845, allowing the Creeks to set aside a tract of land for the Seminoles.

In 1868, the Seminole Nation in Indian Territory was formally established with a capital at Wewoka, Oklahoma. A chief was elected by majority vote. There was also a council consisting of forty-two men. John F. Brown was elected chief. He governed them for over thirty peaceful years. They soon became known as the most peaceful and law-abiding Indian nation in the United States.

Hiding in the Everglades

In August 1842, the war was declared over. There were about 300 Seminoles still hiding in the Everglades of Florida who had not moved to Oklahoma. Living like hunted animals, they were ready to flee at a moment's notice or fight to the death. The United States decided it was not worth the effort to find and capture these remaining Indians.

It was a difficult life for these Indians. They frequently moved their campsites. Encountering soldiers was their greatest worry. Mothers sometimes hid their small children in pits and would only visit them at night. They ate animals, birds, and fish. The Seminoles went deep into the Everglades and lived on islands in the swamps.

In 1855, a party of surveyors came upon Chief Bowleg's village in the Everglades. They destroyed his gardens and stole his crops. Soon the Indians were on the warpath again fighting what is sometimes called the Third Seminole War. The fighting lasted three years. Chief Bowlegs finally agreed to move with one hundred twenty-three men, women, and children to the Indian Territory.

The United States spent more money on the Seminole Wars than any other Indian war. The total cost of the war is estimated to be about $40 million. More than 1,500 soldiers were killed. Yet the Seminole Wars did not bring a clearcut victory for the United States.

Several hundred Seminoles still refused to leave their Florida homeland. They had signed no treaty, and they were unconquered. Staying well hidden in the Everglades, they did not encourage or welcome visitors. They made do with

(Photo courtesy The St. Lucie County Historical Museum)

Chief Billy Bowlegs

very little. The white man finally left them in peace. These people were the ancestors of the Seminoles who live in Florida today. Many Seminoles were killed or removed, but the ones who remained to the bitter end found freedom at last in the vast Florida Everglades.

Between the Seminole Wars and the 1950s

As the surviving Florida Seminoles fled deeper and deeper into the wild swampland, they met an environment that they were not used to. The southern Florida Everglades is lonely and deserted. It is also a place of great beauty. Tall palms, cypress trees, giant ferns, beautiful flowers, birds, and butterflies were abundant. In the forest lived many species of animal life, including the panther and bear. The Seminoles had to learn how to get along with alligators, crocodiles, poisonous snakes, and scorpions. Mosquitoes were everywhere. It was not an easy life.

The Indians abandoned the log house for a more practical shelter called a chickee. The chickee was open on all four sides so the breezes could blow through. It was built on a platform about three feet from the ground. The thatched roof was made of cabbage palms. If the family had to move on quickly, it was easy to abandon.

The raised platform kept a family and its belongings dry when it rained. Crawling insects and snakes could not get in. The Indians' animals could seek shelter under the platform. There was no furniture. Families hung their possessions from cypress rafters and slept on mats on the floor. Babies slept in their own hammocks. During the day, the people sat on the floor eating, sewing, playing games and doing other activities.

Small villages of chickees were built on clumps of higher ground called hammocks. This was the only dry land in the swamp. These villages were well hidden. The Seminoles wanted to stay clear of the white man. Adults spoke in soft, low voices. Children were trained to play quietly without yelling or screaming. They worked together to survive in their new environment.

The small amount of land that was usable was cleared for gardens. The Seminoles planted corn, sweet potatoes, pumpkins, sugar cane, and beans. Gardens had to be carefully guarded against birds and animals. The Seminoles also ate the wild plants around them. Most parts of the palmetto palm was used for food. The leaves were pounded into flour, and molasses was made from the berries. Cattail roots were eaten raw, cooked, or pounded into flour. The coontie root, when mashed and dried, provided a flour for a favorite bread. There were bananas, oranges, pineapples, and coconuts. Hickory nuts were eaten and used for cooking oil. They ate fish and wild game, but killed only what they needed for food.

Another staple food was sofkee. It is a mush made from corn pounded into coarse grains. This is still a popular food today among the Seminoles. A pot of this mixture was kept on the fire all day. Anytime they felt hungry, Indians would dip into the pot with a sofkee spoon.

Food was cooked over an unusual fire. Large logs were arranged into the shape of a spoke. In the middle was a pile of kindling. As the center of the spoke burned, the logs were pushed in. This kept the fire alive. The unburned ends made good benches.

Meat was often cooked on sticks held over an open fire. Other times it was boiled in a large kettle with other foods to make a stew. Sometimes the cooked food was placed on large palm fronds or in shell dishes. There were no individual plates or bowls, but the Seminoles did use shells for drinking cups and knives.

In each village, one or more of the huts was built to serve as a cooking house. Part of the hut was floorless so that the fire could be built on bare ground. The other part of the hut was built for food storage. But, in the hot, damp climate, most food had to be used right away.

Clothing in a Warm Climate

The heavy buckskin and leather clothing that the Seminoles had worn in the northern Florida climate proved too warm in southern Florida. So the Indians adopted long, loose-fitting garments. They used cloth that they got from traders. The presence of mosquitoes and other insects made it necessary to wear clothing that covered most of the body. The women wore long skirts with cape-like blouses. The men wore smock-like long shirts that extended to the knees. An additional part of a man's outfit consisted of two bandannas around his neck and a turban with large feathers on his head. The clothes were decorated with stripes of colored braid and designs cut out of cloth that were sewn around the borders of the skirts. Children dressed the same as their parents. Everyone went barefoot.

Strands of beads worn around the neck were a distinctive part of a woman's costume. When a girl was born, a string of beads was placed around her neck. At significant times in her life, she received additional strands. They were added until the beads covered her neck up to her ears and chin. A woman often wore twenty-five pounds of beads, so that she could barely move her head. The beads became an important part of her outfit. She felt undressed without them. After middle age, women removed the strands one by one until only the first remained. This last strand went to the grave with its wearer.

Seminole men had their hair shaved off except for one crest across the front of their head and another down the top. The women wore their hair loose or in a knot in early times. Fads for hairdos changed from time to time. During one period, a woman's hair was carefully combed over a frame in such a way that it resembled a lopsided visor. That was practical, since it shaded her face from the hot sun.

Shortly after 1900, Seminole clothing was transformed by the introduction of the sewing machine. The braid and print designs sewn on by hand began to disappear. Brightly colored cloth was cut into squares. With the aid of the sewing machine, it was sewn together into intricate and delicate designs. The sewing machine became a necessary part of every household. Clothing was a work of art made entirely out of patchwork. Each dress and shirt was unique. The range of designs was astonishing. The Seminoles got their ideas for designs by studying patterns on the Florida shells and tree snails. They were also inspired by lightning and ocean waves.

To this day, distinctive clothing has become a trademark of the Seminole tribe. Older people can still be seen in more traditional outfits, but modern clothing is worn by the younger generation.

The Seminole Society

The old Creek political system of town chiefs and tribal councils did not work after the Seminole Wars. There were not enough people to run this kind of government. With small, scattered camps, there was little need for formal government. The only remnant of the old system was Court Day during the Green Corn Dance. This festival was held once a year. Crimes against individuals or the group were judged and punishments assigned at this time. Each clan had councilmen representing them in the governing body at the Green Corn Dance.

The clan and the camp are basic social units of the Seminole people. Usually, several closely related families live in one camp. A clan is a group of related families. Each clan had a name: the Panther, Wildcat, Bird, Otter, Wind, Wolf, Snake, and Town clans, among others. A requirement of marriage is to choose a person from another clan.

When a woman wished to attract a husband, she began to wear more beads and silver ornaments on her blouse. Sometimes her family chose her husband. When a couple felt ready to marry, they consulted the leader of the woman's clan. If no one objected, they were married at the Green Corn Dance.

The woman was considered head of the household. After the marriage, the man went to his bride's hut to live. The couple usually lived with the bride's family for a few years. Later the couple started a new camp. The groom provided blankets, cooking utensils, beads, and money, which was turned over to the bride's clan. Divorce was rare, and moral standards were high.

Children were born into the mother's clan, not the father's. Their education was mostly in the hands of the mother

Chief Billy Bowlegs and his family. Even though the climate in Florida is warm, the Seminoles wore clothing that covered their bodies almost completely to protect them from ferocious mosquitos.

(Photo courtesy The St. Lucie County Historical Museum)

and her brothers. Seminole babies wore a small bag of fragrant herbs around their necks to ward off evil spirits and keep the child in good health. The baby slept in a hammock, which the mother kept in motion while she worked. When they were very young, the children were taught how to survive in their environment. They learned to watch for poisonous snakes and insects and other wild creatures.

After the Seminole Wars, the children were taught to play quietly so they would not draw the white man's attention to the camp. The children played many games. They were taught that they must never try to outdo or excel over another. Players tried to help one another. There was no rivalry. This lack of competitiveness is a trait that runs through the entire culture.

At a young age, boys learned to hunt, fish, pole the dugout canoes, and even to make them. At twelve, they were considered men and had all the rights and privileges of any man in the village. Little girls learned how to sew, cook, and take care of babies. By age 14, a girl was generally very accomplished at these tasks and ready for marriage.

Transportation in the Everglades

In northern Florida the Seminoles traveled on foot, on horseback, or by oxcart. There was an elaborate set of trails for visiting and hunting. As the Seminoles moved into terrain dominated by water, boats became all-important. Soon the Indians knew the waterways of the swamps as well as they had once known the land paths. They became skillful navigators.

The Indians learned to make graceful dug-out canoes, the oldest type of boat in the world. The Seminoles carved the boats from large cypress trees that had fallen in the forest. They peeled off the bark and hollowed out the trunk by using burning embers. The charred wood was scraped away with metal blades or with sharp shells.

A boat builder worked slowly, giving the wood time to season. Usually a dugout required several months to construct. It would be used by several generations, passing from father to son. Each family decorated its dugout with the family's distinctive colors. The canoes were used for hunting and transporting goods to the trading post. Whole families rode in them to visit other camps.

These canoes were wider and shallower than the bark canoes of Northern tribes. They had a flat bottom so they could be poled through the shallow water of the Everglades. In the front, the dugout came to a graceful point so that it rose out of the water. The boats floated with perfect balance, skimming through the water with ease. With the help of a mast and sail, some Indians and blacks ventured to Cuba and the Bahamas in these boats.

Today the art of building a dugout has almost disappeared. The automobile and airboat have replaced it. An old boat builder, Charlie Cypress, agreed to make one last canoe. His finished dugout now may be seen in the National Museum of the Smithsonian Institution in Washington, D.C.

Seminole graves.
(Photo courtesy The St. Lucie County Historical Museum)

Religion and Medicine

The Seminoles believe that they do not have a right to harm wild creatures except to obtain food. They reason that other living beings came before man, and that the earth was their home before the Indians arrived. They do not take more than they need from the environment.

Believing that there is no separation between body, mind, and soul, the Seminoles do not make a distinction between religion and medicine. Some illnesses are thought to be produced by spirits or by foreign objects. Others result from a direct relationship between dreams and sickness.

The medicine man used to be a very important person in the tribe. Ceremonies used at times of birth or death, or when a child became an adult, were conducted by the medicine man. He healed the sick. He believed he could control nature and make diseases yield to his efforts.

Treatment included the use of herbal medicines and special healing ceremo-
nies. When someone was sick, the medicine man decided what was causing the illness. The necessary herbs were gathered and mixed into medicine. To drive away the disease spirits, he sang the proper songs and blew on the medicine with a cane tube. His chants were accompanied by drums, bells, and rattles. These were essential because of the Seminole belief that spirits were attracted to noise. He also interpreted a patient's dreams and used that information to guide his treatment plan.

Learning to be a medicine man was a special privilege. Only certain boys were selected. They had to be willing to study long and hard for seven years. Recognizing and gathering plants was part of their education. They learned to mix medicine. Then the rituals of spiritual healing were taught. It was a lifetime occupation, and a medicine man might be quite old before he had complete knowledge.

The medicine man also supervised bury-

23

ing the dead. Seminoles were buried in a remote place in the swamp or woods. Usually the body was placed in a coffin which was placed above the ground under a thatched shelter. All of the deceased's possessions were buried with the body. The Seminoles believed the departed would need his or her tools in the afterlife. The possessions had to be broken first because that was the only way they could accompany the dead person to heaven. Guns, knives, even pots and pans were bent out of shape before they were placed with the body.

Today, most Indians are buried in cemeteries. Missionaries have been active in Florida for a long time. The majority of Seminoles on the reservations are Christian, mostly Baptist or Methodist. Small frame churches are found on each of the reservations. One of the most famous medicine men was converted to Christianity during the period of World War II, and he was helpful in converting many other Seminoles. Because Indian traditions and Christian ideas do not mix well, the Indian religion is disappearing.

Most of the Seminoles living away from the reservations have not adopted the Christian faith. Their isolation has kept alive their mistrust of the white man and his ways. It is hard for Seminoles to believe that everything their ancestors believed and practiced is now false. They hesitate to be converted completely. Overall, the Seminoles have a high tolerance for other religions. Often their solution to Christianity is to blend it with the old beliefs.

Even though living in one of the wild-

est and roughest regions of the United States, the Seminoles' health is surprisingly good. They are far healthier than most of the other American tribes. They are a hardy people who have adapted to their environment. Fresh air and lots of physical exercise are two factors. Each family is isolated from the next. Their freedom to manage their own affairs is important. Older people are highly respected. Many of the people live long lives because they believe in the inevitable and do not spend their time worrying.

One chronic medical problem over the years has been hookworm. Because the people like to go barefoot, they are more susceptible to the infection. Today many Seminole women are overweight. When this condition is combined with a starchy, sugary diet, it often leads to diabetes. In recent years, their closer association with the white man has brought various contagious diseases into the tribe. Measles, chicken pox, and mumps have been some of the problem diseases. Innoculation programs at modern clinics are helping to eliminate these diseases.

In 1979 the Seminole tribe began a new health program for the people. The program has made progress in meeting the health needs of the Seminole people. Today Seminoles use modern health clinics and, if necessary, hospitals. The infant death rate is now lower, because most pregnant women have their babies in the hospital. Walk-in dental services are provided. The medicine man is still consulted for certain illnesses, but slowly the modern doctor and modern medicine is taking over.

Green Corn Dance

The most important Seminole ceremony is the Green Corn Dance. Like other traditions, the Green Corn Dance is dying out. Today, younger people regard it more lightly, paying less attention to the rules.

Traditionally, the Green Corn Dance was held when the corn was ripe and was also the Seminole New Year celebration. This festival derives from the Seminole's Creek ancestry. The celebration ran from four to eight days. The medicine man and his assistants chose the actual date and location. An effort was made to keep the special ceremonies secret from outsiders. The Seminoles wanted privacy.

The dance served various functions for the tribe. It was a time for all members to be purged of uncleanliness and to be healed. Marriages or divorces could be granted or refused. Tribal business of the past year was transacted. The festival was also a time of spiritual renewal. Children learned their religious obligations. Boys of thirteen to fifteen received a new name. The name was chosen by their

elders or by the medicine man and symbolized adulthood.

The medicine bundle was an important part of the medicine man's healing services. Before the Green Corn Dance began, the medicine man bathed himself and prayed that he would handle the bundle wisely and for the good of all. This packet was very sacred. It was only brought out of hiding at the Green Corn Dance. The Seminoles believed that the medicine in the bundle was given to them from God and contained everything necessary for the Indians' well-being. The medicine itself consisted of 600 to 700 bits of horn, feathers, stones, herbs, dried animal parts, and other items. When folded up, the deerskin package was about one foot by two feet long and five or six inches thick. In earlier times during war, smaller bundles were sent with the warriors to give them power and protection.

An important rite of the festival was the drinking of a mystic black brew made from the leaves of various plants. The brew was believed to cleanse the body internally and purify the people from all bad thoughts and acts. It also gave warriors extra strength and power. Only the men were allowed to drink the brew.

Games were played during the Green Corn Dance. The most popular one was stickball, an early form of the modern game of lacrosse. The Seminoles played the game around a 30-foot tree on the dance ground. The object was to hit the tree with a deerskin ball the size of a walnut. The men played against the women, who had the advantage of using their hands. The men had to use spoonlike scoops carved from large pieces of wood.

The festival was a time for feasting and dancing. Old and young sang songs and danced. Not all the dances were of a religious nature. Some were purely for entertainment. Ancestral folk songs from the Green Corn Dance have survived for generations in southern Florida. Musical instruments accompanied the songs: rattles made from coconut and turtle shells, small water drums and tom-toms and sometimes a flute. In more recent times, tin cans pierced with nail holes and containing a few beads or hard seeds replaced the shells.

Seminoles Today

Today Florida Seminoles number about 1,500 people. According to the 1980 census, most live on one of five reservations: 480 acres in Hollywood; 35,000 acres in Brighton, west of Lake Okeechobee; 10 acres near Immokalee; 8.2 acres near Tampa; and the biggest reservation; 70,000 acres at Big Cypress in the southern Everglades.

About 6,000 Seminoles live in Oklahoma. Like any other citizen of that state, their children attend public schools. Many of the Seminoles are farmers, ranchers, teachers, doctors, or civic leaders. In Oklahoma the Indians' customs and traditions have almost completely vanished.

The Seminoles in Florida divide into two distinct groups, the Miccosukees (mi KOS oo keez) and the Cow Creeks, or Muskogees (mus KO gees), as they were also called. Their traits and culture are similar. But their language is so different that they cannot understand each other.

The Muskogees tilled the soil and raised farm animals. They were always more settled and peaceful. Most of the Muskogees allowed themselves to be sent to Oklahoma. In Florida, the ones that stayed now live on the Brighton Reservation.

Two thirds of the Florida Seminoles are the Miccosukees. Many live on Big Cypress in the Everglades. Descended from the Creek warrior tribe, they were traditionally hunters and fishermen. During the Seminole Wars, they provided most of the campaign leaders. Of all the Indian tribes in America, only they can claim to be undefeated. The Miccosukees have held onto their heritage longer than other groups have. For a long time, these Indians resisted learning English or any of the white man's ways.

Modern conveniences are evident in Seminole homes. The cinderblock house has replaced the chickee. Most Seminoles still have a chickee in the yard for picnics and other activities. Seminoles have profited by building chickees for the white man. They are now found on sandy beaches at resorts, beside pools, on golf courses and in back yards. Building chickees for profit has also given the older Seminole a chance to pass the art of chickee building along to the younger men helping them.

Contrasts between old customs and modern ways is interesting. It was not unusual to see a television, electric fan, iron, and mattress in an open-air chickee during the transition period when the Seminoles were moving into modern houses. Today almost all families live in modern houses.

The Seminoles support themselves in many different ways. They work as managers, office workers, and physical laborers. Some run tourist attractions, selling crafts and wrestling alligators. Seminoles used to be happy with their easy-going life. Today younger Seminoles want to live and work like their modern neighbors.

Seminole men still hunt and fish, but

28

they do not contribute a great amount of the family's food. Rarely do the women make their own flour. Seminole women are seen regularly in supermarkets buying modern foods.

The Seminole Tribe of Florida was formally organized and recognized by the federal government in 1957. This meant assistance for much needed services for the people and a future for the tribe. The Seminoles run most affairs for themselves. The tribe used to rely financially on the federal government. Because of successful business ventures, less than half of their budget comes from the government. The Seminoles are citizens of the United States and Florida. They can vote, hold public office, own land and personal property.

The tribe is governed by a five-member council. Each member is elected from one of the reservations. The chief is elected at large. The council is the corporation's board of directors and the chief is its president.

The Seminole tribe has been a leader for other national Indian tribes in business affairs. Because of their ideas, many tribes are trying economic projects. The Seminoles have become shrewd businessmen. Being exempt from state taxes is an advantage of their status as citizens of a federal reservation. The Seminole tribe has various ventures, including cattle raising, bingo halls, tax-free cigarette outlets, and a luxury hotel.

The tribe's share of the profits is used to improve the Seminole's living conditions. Community projects, such as recreational facilities and college scholarships, are top priority. Health, education, and housing programs are also important. Dividends are paid to tribal members every other month.

In 1972, the Seminole Tribe contracted the Bureau of Indian Affairs to establish an Office of Education. The Education Division offers several programs to the people: an early childhood center, a Head Start program, counseling, financial assistance for college, and employment assistance. A vocational program trains Seminoles for jobs. Another special program is designed to teach the children the importance of saving the language, customs, and traditions of the Seminole people.

In the old days, children were educated in the home. Today they are required to attend school until age sixteen. The high school drop-out rate is still very high. Tribal leaders realize the importance of education to the progress of the tribe. They are making every effort to keep young Seminole people in school.

The Seminoles are a proud people. The injustices of the Seminole Wars has made them slow to adapt to white man's society and modern life. Today that is changing, as members of the younger generation accept the ways of their modern neighbors.

Leg rattles made from tin cans, worn for the Green Corn Dance. (Photo courtesy The St. Lucie County Historical Museum)

Important Dates in Seminole History

1513 — Spain begins exploring Florida.

1565 — St. Augustine established.

1600's — Florida Indians in revolt against Spanish rule.

1701 — War of the Spanish Succession, Creek Indians side with British and invade Florida.

1700's — With Florida Indians killed or sold into slavery, Creek invaders settle into Northern Florida. Beginning of Seminole tribe.

1763 — Florida becomes a British Territory. Seminoles firmly established in northern Florida at this time.

1783 — Treaty of Paris returns Florida to Spain.

1818 — Clashes between United States and Spain in Florida lead to First Seminole War.

1819 — Florida ceded to the United States and becomes territory of the United States.

1823 — Settlers move into northern Florida. Seminoles reluctantly agree to give up 32 million acres of land in northern Florida and move to a reservation in central Florida.

1828 — Andrew Jackson is elected President of the United States.

1830 — U.S. Congress passes the Indian Removal Act that forces all Indians to move west of the Mississippi River.

1835 — Osceola speaks for the Seminoles saying they refuse to move again. Second Seminole War begins.

1838 — Tricked into a truce, Osceola is captured and thrown into prison where he dies.

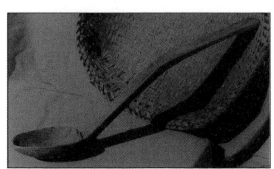

Sofkee spoon.
(Photo courtesy The St. Lucie County Historical Museum)

INDEX

Corn grinder.
(Photo courtesy The St. Lucie County Historical Museum)